UNDERGROUND WORLDS

# ANCIENT UNDERGROUND STRUCTURES

Natalie Hyde

CRABTREE
PUBLISHING COMPANY
WWW.CRABTREEBOOKS.COM

# CRABTREE
## PUBLISHING COMPANY
### WWW.CRABTREEBOOKS.COM

**Author:** Natalie Hyde

**Editorial Director:** Kathy Middleton

**Editors:** Petrice Custance, Sonya Newland

**Proofreaders:** Lorna Notsch, Ellen Rodger

**Designer:** Steve Mead

**Cover design:** Tammy McGarr

**Production coordinator and
    Prepress technician:** Tammy McGarr

**Print coordinator:** Katherine Berti

Produced for Crabtree Publishing Company
by White-Thomson Publishing Ltd

**Photographs**

**Cover:** iStock: SangHyunPaek (top right);
All other images from Shutterstock

**Interior:** Alamy: 5 (David Jones), 15 (Mark Green), 16–17 (Roger
Hollingsworth), 17 (Alan Wrigley), 23 (Julie Woodhouse), 24 (Hemis), 25
(Hemis), 28–29 (National Geographic Creative); Julian Baker: 6, 14, 22;
Getty Images: 4–5 (Insights), 11t (AFP), 11b (AFP), 18 (DEA / A. DAGLI
ORTI/De Agostini), 19 (Universal Images Group), 29 (DEA / P. LIACI);
iStock: 12 (traveler1116); Shutterstock: 6–7 (Nina Lishchuk), 8 (Mikhail
Gnatkovskiy), 9 (Morphart Creation), 10 (Noradoa), 13 (Stefania Valvola),
20 (Anton_Ivanov), 21 (Fotokon), 27t (muratart), 27b (Luciano Mortula –
LGM).

**Library and Archives Canada Cataloguing in Publication**

Hyde, Natalie, 1963-, author
        Ancient underground structures / Natalie Hyde.

(Underground worlds)
Includes index.
Issued in print and electronic formats.
ISBN 978-0-7787-6078-8 (hardcover).--
ISBN 978-0-7787-6128-0 (softcover).--
ISBN 978-1-4271-2247-6 (HTML)

        1. Civilization, Subterranean--Juvenile literature.  2. Underground
architecture--History--To 1500--Juvenile literature.  3. Underground
construction--History--To 1500--Juvenile literature.  I. Title.

GN755.H93 2018            j720'.47309            C2018-905516-2
                                                 C2018-905517-0

**Library of Congress Cataloging-in-Publication Data**

Names: Hyde, Natalie, 1963- author.
Title: Ancient underground structures / Natalie Hyde.
Description: New York, New York : Crabtree Publishing, 2019.
Series: Underground worlds | Includes index.
Identifiers: LCCN 2018043795 (print) | LCCN 2018045978 (ebook) |
  ISBN 9781427122476 (Electronic) |
  ISBN 9780778760788 (hardcover) |
  ISBN 9780778761280 (pbk.)
Subjects: LCSH: Civilization, Subterranean--Juvenile literature. |
  Underground areas--Juvenile literature. | Underground
  architecture--Juvenile literature.
Classification: LCC GN755 (ebook) | LCC GN755 .H94 2019 (print) |
  DDC 624.1/909012--dc23
LC record available at https://lccn.loc.gov/2018043795

## Crabtree Publishing Company

www.crabtreebooks.com              1-800-387-7650

Printed in the U.S.A./122018/CG20181005

**Published in Canada
Crabtree Publishing**
616 Welland Ave.
St. Catharines, Ontario
L2M 5V6

**Published in the United States
Crabtree Publishing**
PMB 59051
350 Fifth Avenue, 59th Floor
New York, New York 10118

**Published in the United Kingdom
Crabtree Publishing**
Maritime House
Basin Road North, Hove
BN41 1WR

**Published in Australia
Crabtree Publishing**
3 Charles Street
Coburg North
VIC, 3058

# CONTENTS

ANCIENT SECRETS ....................................... 4

DERINKUYU, CAPPADOCIA ........................... 6

PARIS CATACOMBS ..................................... 8

TEMPLE OF THE PLUMED SERPENT ............ 10

ORVIETO .................................................. 12

CHAVÍN DE HUÁNTAR ............................... 14

FOGOUS .................................................. 16

HYPOGEUM OF HAL SAFLIENI ................... 18

NUSHABAD ............................................... 20

CITY OF CAVES, NOTTINGHAM .................. 22

CAVES OF NAOURS.................................... 24

THE BASILICA CISTERN ............................. 26

TOMB OF SETI I ....................................... 28

GLOSSARY ................................................ 30

LEARNING MORE ....................................... 31

INDEX ..................................................... 32

# ANCIENT SECRETS

With modern science and technology, most of Earth's surface has been explored. But new secret worlds are still being discovered underground. Humans began building underground structures in the very distant past. Some ancient sites belowground date back as far as 1500 B.C.E.

## Underground Spaces

Burial places, tunnels, chambers, and workshops were created beneath fields and cities. Later, they may have had different uses, such as storerooms or shelters during times of war. Over the centuries, many of them were lost. But now we are rediscovering our past. As we uncover these long-forgotten places, we learn how our **ancestors** lived and survived. Ancient underground structures can be found all over the world.

▷ The ancient temple complex at Chavín de Huántar in Peru (see pages 14–15) includes a maze of underground tunnels and chambers.

## Different Places, Different Uses

Some sites began as natural caves. Others were first used for one purpose, such as a mine, but then had a second purpose, such as a bomb shelter. It is amazing to think that such large and complex structures were built or extended with hand tools. Some spaces are beautifully decorated. Others have clever security features to protect the people inside from attack. All of them show how **resourceful** our ancestors were.

△ The tunnels beneath Naours in France (see pages 24–25) have been used as a hiding place and a headquarters in times of war for centuries.

# DERINKUYU,
## CAPPADOCIA

Derinkuyu is a town with a deep secret. All through history, the Cappadocia region of Turkey was an important trade zone between Asia and Europe, which made it a target for attacks. To protect themselves from invading armies, the people of Cappadocia went underground.

## Life Underground

Underground Derinkuyu was discovered in 1963, when a man knocked down a wall in his house and found a room underneath. Scientists believe the underground complex is about 3,600 years old. The network of rooms and tunnels includes shops, temples, storerooms, and living quarters. There were even pens for farm animals. Around 15,000 **airshafts** delivered fresh air to this underground space.

A section of the underground city of Derinkuyu ▷

Entrance from the street

**Ventilation** shafts

Rolling stone doors for protection

Underground church

Underground water supply

▽ Residents could live underground comfortably for a long time in Derinkuyu.

## DID YOU KNOW?

The volcanic rock of this area **eroded** to create large stone pillars or cones. These are called "fairy chimneys," and people carved homes into them.

## Staying Safe

Everything about the underground structure was designed for protection. Huge round stones could be rolled across doorways to block them. These could only be moved from inside the complex. There were also several water wells. That was so that the people inside would always have clean water, even if invaders decided to poison one of the wells.

# PARIS CATACOMBS

If you walk the streets of Paris, France, chances are you will be walking on graves! The **catacombs** of Paris are a network of underground tunnels. They are now famous as burial places, but they started out with a different purpose.

## Roman Roots

The catacombs date back to ancient Roman times, when they were created as **limestone** mines. The Romans used limestone to build arenas, monuments, and **bathhouses**. After the end of the Roman Empire, in around 476 C.E., the tunnels lay unused for centuries.

## Running Out of Room

In the late 1700s, Paris had a problem. Its burial grounds were overcrowded, and some bodies were not buried safely. This created a health risk for people living in the city. In 1786, workers began moving all the bones from the city's main cemetery, Holy Innocents, to the empty mine tunnels, turning them into catacombs.

Signs in the catacombs mark which ▷ cemetery the bones came from.

△ People have been able to take tours of the catacombs since the 1800s.

## Moving Bones

Over the next 80 years, bones from other cemeteries were relocated to the tunnels. The human remains were always moved at night. They were placed on carts and covered in a black cloth. The carts moved in a **procession**, led by priests.

In 1814, part of the catacombs was opened to the public. It still is today. Visitors can walk along the galleries lined with stacks of bones. Some are arranged in patterns, and others are piled up to create pillars.

## DID YOU KNOW?

People have always been curious about the catacombs—even royalty! The future French king Charles X toured them in 1787, and Napoleon III visited in 1860.

# TEMPLE OF THE
# PLUMED SERPENT

In 2003, heavy rains at the ancient **Mayan** site of Teotihuacan in Mexico uncovered a tunnel under the Temple of the Plumed Serpent. **Archaeologist** Sergio Gomez began **excavating** to find out what it was, where it went, and what it was for.

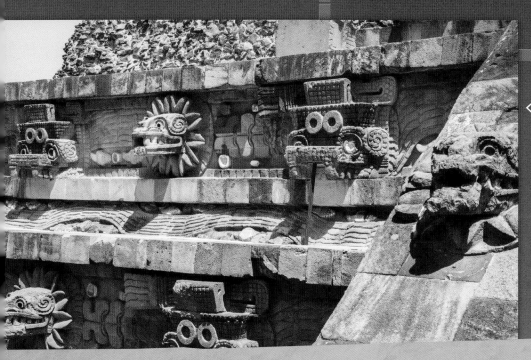

◁ The Temple of the Plumed Serpent gets its name from the carvings on the outside, which may represent the god Quetzalcoatl.

## Starry Night

What Gomez discovered was a **sacred** place, full of treasures. One of the first things he noticed was pieces of **pyrite** stuck into the rocks in the tunnel. When he turned all lights and lamps off, the pieces of pyrite glowed. They looked like stars in the sky. The people who put them there may have been representing the universe. Gomez and his team also found necklaces, boxes of beetle wings, pottery with powdery corn inside, knives, and figurines. One little statue looks like a jaguar ready to pounce.

## Guardians of the Dead?

At the end of the tunnel, right beneath the center of the temple, Gomez found a cross-shaped chamber. Two carved black statues stood guard at its entrance. Below these statues lie three more chambers, but they have not been opened yet. They may be burial chambers for the powerful kings of Teotihuacan. In 2017, another mysterious tunnel was found beneath a different temple at Teotihuacan.

△ Sergio Gomez, shown here in the tunnel beneath the Temple of the Plumed Serpent, believes the artifacts were offerings to the gods.

## DID YOU KNOW?

Progress is often slow during archaeological digs. because workers use small brushes to carefully clear away the dirt. This is so they don't damage any hidden **artifacts**.

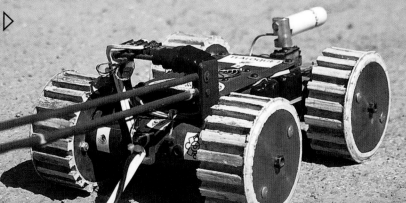

Robot cameras are being ▷ used to explore the parts of the tunnels that workers can't reach.

# ORVIETO

The city of Orvieto lies on a volcanic **bluff** in southwestern Italy. It was founded by a group of ancient peoples called Etruscans. For safety, the residents created workshops and wells underground in the volcanic rock.

## Well, Well, Well

Having a community on top of a bluff has its advantages. The people of Orvieto could see for miles around, so they could keep watch for invaders heading their way. The cliffs offered protection if anyone got too close. But there are also disadvantages. Orvieto's water source was located far away on the **plains** below the bluff. To solve this problem, residents came up with an idea. They dug into the rock and created **cisterns** to catch and store rainwater.

▽ The tunnels under Orvieto were used during **World War II** to seek shelter from bombs.

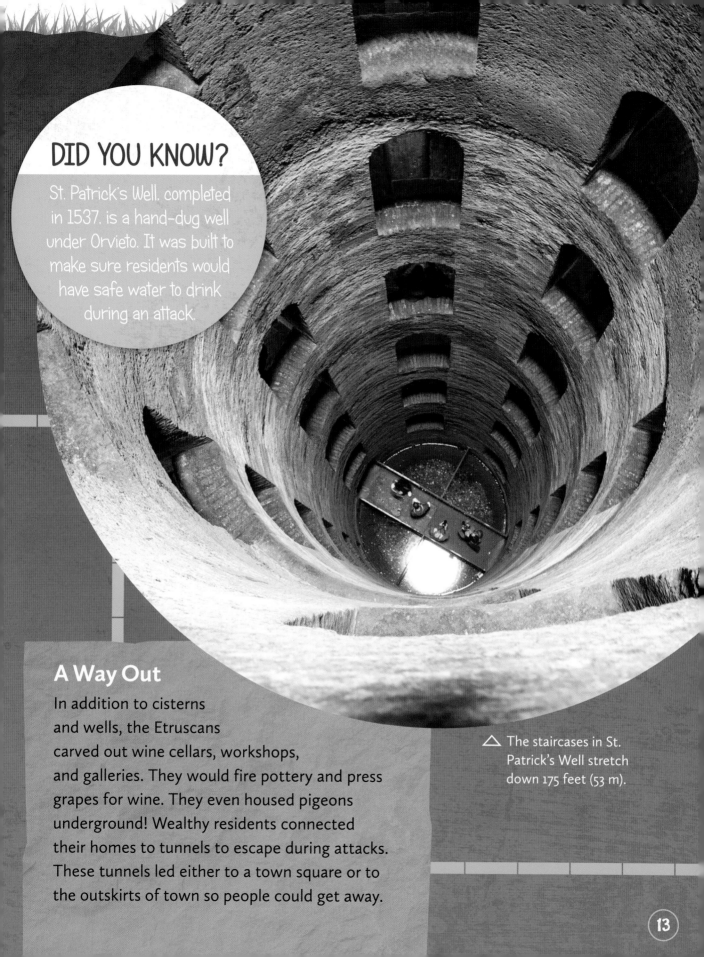

## DID YOU KNOW?

St. Patrick's Well, completed in 1537, is a hand-dug well under Orvieto. It was built to make sure residents would have safe water to drink during an attack.

## A Way Out

In addition to cisterns and wells, the Etruscans carved out wine cellars, workshops, and galleries. They would fire pottery and press grapes for wine. They even housed pigeons underground! Wealthy residents connected their homes to tunnels to escape during attacks. These tunnels led either to a town square or to the outskirts of town so people could get away.

△ The staircases in St. Patrick's Well stretch down 175 feet (53 m).

# CHAVÍN DE HUÁNTAR

The Chavín peoples lived in the Andes Mountains of Peru around 900–200 B.C.E. They left behind an amazing temple complex called Chavín de Huántar. It has been named a **UNESCO World Heritage Site**.

## Holy Place

Chavín de Huántar was a place of worship. People traveled from far and wide to visit the temples and make offerings there. The ancient complex has stone terraces, plazas, carvings, and temples. But what archaeologists found underground is even more amazing. Beneath the temples around the plaza is a maze of tunnels and galleries.

▽ A plan of the Chavín de Huántar temple complex

The Old Temple was built around 1000 B.C.E.

The New Temple was built between 500–200 B.C.E. and is in the shape of a flat-topped pyramid with two chapels on top.

Beneath the U-shaped Old Temple is the gallery of the Lanzón.

The walls of the sunken courtyard were decorated with carved heads of men and animals.

14

## The Lanzón

The Chavín tunnels are believed to have been very holy places used only by priests. At one point where several tunnels meet, there is a carved column. It is 15 feet (4.6 m) tall and known as the Lanzón. Carved on the Lanzón is a figure that is half beast, half human. Scientists believe the use of fangs, claws, and serpent eyebrows shows the importance of animals such as jaguars, **caiman**, and snakes to the Chavín peoples.

◁ Lanzón means "great spear" in Spanish.

# FOGOUS

The fogous of Cornwall, in southern England, are full of mystery. These underground spaces were built during the **Iron Age**, in around 800 B.C.E. But even experts are not sure what they were used for.

## Hiding in Plain Sight

Fogou means "cave" in Cornish. About 15 fogous have been found. They were built by humans in the form of trenches lined with stones. When a trench had been dug, large rock slabs were laid over the top to form a roof. This was covered with earth and grasses to make the fogous almost invisible. Some experts believe this allowed people to hide from attackers. Bones and pieces of pottery found in the fogous suggest they might have been used to store food, such as grains or gull eggs.

▽ The remains of the Iron Age village of Carn Euny include a stone-walled fogou.

## DID YOU KNOW?

Halliggye Fogou has found a new purpose in recent years. It has become the winter hibernation site for **endangered** horseshoe bats.

## Famous Fogous

The largest of these cave complexes is the Halliggye Fogou. It has a 66-foot (20-m) passageway leading to three chambers. Another fogou, Boleigh Fogou, is accessed by a creepway. This is a small narrow passage too low for an adult to stand up in. Pendeen Fogou is said to be haunted. Locals say a lady in white stands near the entrance and that it is bad luck to see her.

△ Halligge Fogou was part of a small farming settlement. This is a passage entrance in the fogou.

# HYPOGEUM OF HAL SAFLIENI

In 1902, workers building some new houses in Paola, Malta, got a big surprise. They accidentally cut through the roof of an underground temple. This is now known as the Hypogeum of Hal Saflieni. Hypogeum means "underground chamber" in Latin.

## Place of the Dead

The hypogeum was a huge underground cemetery, built around 2500 B.C.E. Archaeologists have found more than 7,000 bodies there. They also found many beautiful artifacts in the burial tombs, including shell buttons, beads, and small stone and clay figures. Some of these figurines may have been worn as pendants on necklaces.

## Interior Design

The entire hypogeum is underground. The entrance would originally have been at street level, but only a few blocks remain to show where that was. Belowground, there are three levels. Some are natural caves, and other spaces are carved out of limestone. Despite the simple tools available at the time, these rooms aren't just rough, rounded holes—they are very detailed. Many of the walls and ceilings are decorated with designs and colored with a paint made of a crushed rock called red ochre.

▽ Amazingly, the rooms were carved out using only simple stone tools and deer antlers for digging. These were the only tools available at the time.

▽ The Stone Age "Sleeping Lady" figure is made from a clay called terra-cotta.

### DID YOU KNOW?

The "Sleeping Lady" figure is an amazing piece of art. The carving is so detailed that experts were able to determine how real furniture, such as the couch, was made at the time.

# NUSHABAD

To survive in a desert, you need water and shelter from the heat. Ancient people in Iran knew that the best place to find both was underground. In 2004, a man digging a sewage ditch in Nushabad, Iran, discovered evidence of this ancient underground lifestyle in the form of an incredible buried complex.

## Stop for a Drink

Legend says that 1,500 years ago, a king in ancient Iran stopped by a desert well to drink. He found the water so refreshing that he ordered a settlement to be built around the well. He named the city Nushabad, which means "city of cold tasty water." The city includes three underground levels of tunnels, chambers, air vents, staircases, and canals.

▽ Entrances to the tunnels could be found inside some homes, as well as in public places aboveground.

## Safety First

Nushabad was a vital shelter for residents to protect themselves from enemies. They built in special safety features, including **booby traps**. For example, holes were built into some floors and then covered with stones. If someone stepped on them, they would fall through. Underground, each family had its own rooms. People had everything they needed to stay hidden for some weeks, including water.

▽ Narrow tunnels and steep staircases made it difficult for invaders to move around once inside.

## DID YOU KNOW?

The doorways into the complex were purposely built small and narrow. This forced an enemy army to enter one at a time. Those inside could then easily attack the invaders.

# CITY OF CAVES,
## NOTTINGHAM

In 1330, King Edward III and a group of supporters crept through a tunnel into Nottingham Castle, in England. They took a man named Roger Mortimer prisoner for stealing the throne from Edward's father. This daring deed was only possible because of the ancient network of caves and passageways under the city.

## Out of Sight

The tunnel King Edward and his supporters used was later named Mortimer's Hole. It is one of more than 544 caves and passageways that have existed in this "City of Caves" in Nottingham for more than 1,000 years. The caves had many uses over the centuries. The remains of an underground **tannery** were found, which means some caves were used as workshops. Tanning required the use of dung, or poop, making the tannery so smelly that even rats stayed away!

▽ Part of the cave system beneath Nottingham

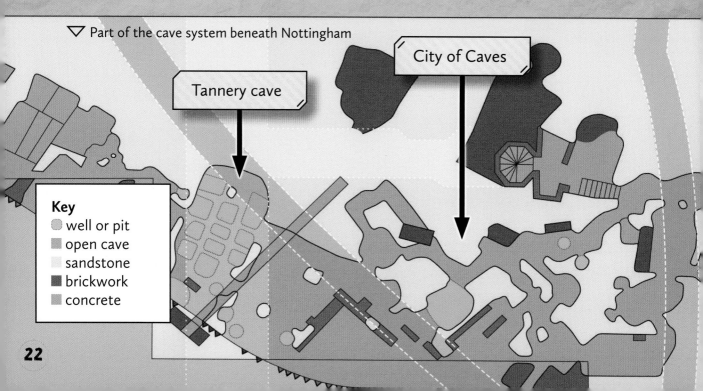

City of Caves

Tannery cave

**Key**
- well or pit
- open cave
- sandstone
- brickwork
- concrete

22

△ The caves have existed since at least 868 C.E., when they were mentioned in the writings of a Welsh monk.

## No Place to Live

When Nottingham grew overcrowded in the 1800s, people started renting the caves to those who couldn't find anywhere to live. Often, entire families lived in one room. With no fresh air and no bathrooms, it was not a pleasant experience. Diseases spread quickly and easily. During World War II, the tunnels and rooms were used as air-raid shelters. New caves and tunnels are still being found in Nottingham today.

## DID YOU KNOW?

Legend has it that Robin Hood even used these tunnels to get in and out of Nottingham Castle!

# CAVES OF NAOURS

During World War II, many parts of Europe were destroyed by bombs. The only safe place was in a **bunker**. Often, residents used existing underground spaces to stay safe. Sometimes the enemy used them, too.

## Storage and Safety

The underground network of tunnels and rooms under the town of Naours, France, was one such place. The cave and tunnel system here began as a limestone **quarry** in ancient Roman times. Later, people realized that it was ideal for storage and shelter. During the Thirty Years' War (1618–48) and later conflicts, the area was often raided by armies looking for supplies. The tunnels were a safe place for people to hide from invading armies.

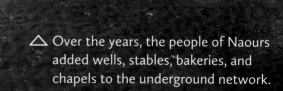

△ Over the years, the people of Naours added wells, stables, bakeries, and chapels to the underground network.

## DID YOU KNOW?

The chimneys for oven fires belowground were routed through the cottages above. This hid the fact that people were hiding in the caves below.

▽ Today, the caves are open to the public. Visitors can see the largest collection of **graffiti** from **World War I** in the world.

## William Was Here

When peace returned to Naours, the tunnel network was forgotten and was not rediscovered until 1887. During World War I (1914–18), soldiers would visit the tunnels and leave notes and signatures on the walls. During World War II, when the Germans invaded France, they used the caves as their regional headquarters.

# THE BASILICA CISTERN

In the 1500s, there were tales of people in Constantinople (now Istanbul) being able to pull fresh water and even fish from holes in their basements. When a visitor to the city went to investigate, he found it was true.

## Beauty Underground

He discovered a huge, underground cistern. This had been built by the Romans in 532 C.E. but had later been forgotten. It is said that 7,000 enslaved people built the cistern. One of the marble pillars in the cistern has carvings of tears. Legend says these tears were for the hundreds of people who died while building the cistern. There were fish swimming in the fresh water there. It was so beautifully decorated that people called it the "Sunken Palace."

## Water World

The cistern supplied water to the Great Palace of Constantinople and other buildings nearby. In the past, when the water was still deep, people could explore the cistern in rowboats. Today, the water is only a few feet deep. But visitors can use a raised walkway with modern lighting to explore this amazing underground space.

The cistern has 336 carved marble pillars holding up a **vaulted** brick ceiling.

△ The Medusa bases may have been moved to the cistern from an ancient Roman building.

# TOMB OF SETI I

The Valley of the Kings is a desert valley in Egypt that contains many tombs of the ancient Egyptian **pharaohs**. In 1817, a man named Giovanni Belzoni was digging in the valley when he uncovered the entrance to a previously unknown tomb.

## Breaking and Entering

Experts later realized that this was the tomb of pharaoh Seti I, who ruled from 1290 to 1279 B.C.E. It was one of the most beautifully decorated tombs ever discovered. At the time, however, Belzoni did not know exactly what he had found. He was not an archaeologist, and as he dug, he damaged parts of the precious tomb. Some of the paint and the wall carvings were removed by accident.

▽ Inside the tomb of Seti I

Burial chamber with **astronomical** paintings on the ceiling

Hall of Pillars

Hall where a **mummified** bull was found

Chamber with a bench around the walls to hold funeral items

## The Missing Pharaoh

Inside the tomb was a **sarcophagus**, but there was no body in it. Pharaohs were buried with a great deal of treasure, which meant there was always a risk of grave robbers. Priests had removed Seti's body and hidden it so that it would not be harmed. When Belzoni entered the tomb, he saw pieces of wooden furniture and mummified animals. All the jewels and other valuable items were gone.

## Painted Stories

Later explorers removed some wall panels, which are now in museums around the world. The painted walls that remain in the tomb are among the finest surviving examples of ancient Egyptian art. Decorations once covered every passageway and chamber in Seti's tomb. Even the ceiling in the burial chamber was painted with **constellations** in the night sky.

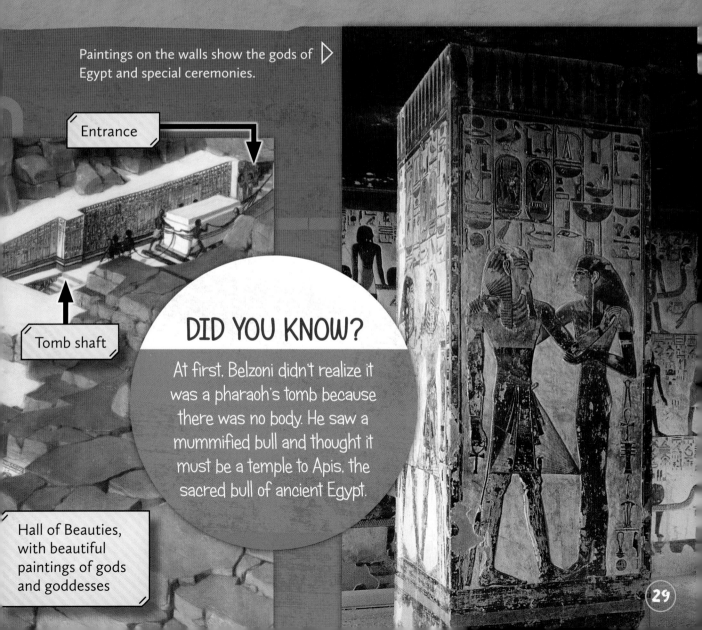

Paintings on the walls show the gods of ▷ Egypt and special ceremonies.

Entrance

Tomb shaft

### DID YOU KNOW?

At first, Belzoni didn't realize it was a pharaoh's tomb because there was no body. He saw a mummified bull and thought it must be a temple to Apis, the sacred bull of ancient Egypt.

Hall of Beauties, with beautiful paintings of gods and goddesses

# GLOSSARY

**airshaft** A vertical opening that lets fresh air into a sealed-off space

**ancestor** A relative from the past

**archaeologist** Someone who studies human history

**artifact** An object that has been made by humans

**astronomical** Describes things relating to astronomy, such as stars and planets

**bathhouse** A community building where citizens can bathe

**bluff** A steep bank or cliff

**booby trap** A trick designed to surprise or harm someone

**bunker** An underground shelter for use in wartime

**caiman** A reptile similar to a small crocodile

**catacombs** Underground cemeteries

**cistern** A tank for storing water

**constellation** A pattern of stars in the night sky

**endangered** At risk of becoming extinct, or dying out

**eroded** Worn away by wind or water

**excavating** Removing earth by digging

**graffiti** Writing or drawing on a public wall

**Iron Age** A period of history from about 800 B.C.E. to the first century C.E.

**limestone** A type of soft rock, often used for buildings

**Maya** An ancient civilization in Central America

**mummified** A dead body preserved by covering in oil and wrapping in cloth

**pharaoh** A ruler in ancient Egypt

**plain** A large area of flat land without many trees

**pope** The leader of the Roman Catholic Church

**procession** A march or parade

**pyrite** A shiny yellow mineral

**quarry** A place where rock, stone, or other natural substances are dug out of the ground

**resourceful** Clever at finding ways to make use of things around you

**sacred** Describes something that has religious importance

**sarcophagus** A stone coffin

**tannery** A place where leather is made

**UNESCO World Heritage Site**
A site selected by the United Nations Educational, Scientific, and Cultural Organization as being historically important

**vaulted** Arched

**ventilation** The movement of fresh air into a room

**World War I** A global conflict that lasted from 1914–1918

**World War II** A global conflict that lasted from 1939–1945

# LEARNING MORE

## Books

Arnold, Caroline, *City of the Gods: Mexico's Ancient City of Teotihuacan.* StarWalk Kids, 2013.

Baby Professor, *Who Lived in Peru before the Inca Empire?* Speedy Publishing, 2017.

Berger, Melvin, *Mummies of the Pharaohs: Exploring the Valley of the Kings.* National Geographic Children's Books, 2001.

## Websites

**https://kids.kiddle.co/Teotihuac%C3%A1n**
Learn more about the ancient site of Teotihuacan.

**www.limaeasy.com/lima-info/lima-history-and-cultures/the-chavin-culture-1200bc-200ad**
See some great images of Chavin culture artifacts from Peru.

**https://news.nationalgeographic.com/2015/03/150325-underground-city-cappadocia-turkey-archaeology/**
Watch a laser-scan video inside Derinkuyu, Turkey, with National Geographic.

# INDEX

artifacts  10, 11, 18, 19

Basilica Cistern  26–27
Belzoni, Giovanni  28, 29
bomb shelters  5, 23
booby traps  21

caves  5, 16, 17, 19, 22, 23, 24, 25
cemeteries  8, 9, 18
Charles X  9
Chavin de Huantar  4, 14–15
cisterns  12, 13, 26, 27
City of Caves, Nottingham  22–23

Derinkuyu  6–7

Edward III  22
enemy invasions  6, 7, 12, 13, 16, 21, 24
Etruscans  12, 13

fogous  16–17

Gomez, Sergio  10, 11
graffiti  25

Hypogeum of Hal Saflieni  18–19

Iron Age  16

Mayan peoples  10
Medusa  27
mines  5, 8
Mortimer, Roger  22

Naours  5, 24–25
Napoleon III  9
Nottingham Castle  22, 23
Nushabad  20–21

Orvieto  12–13

Paris catacombs  8–9

pottery  10, 13, 16

Robin Hood  23
Romans  8, 24, 26, 27

Seti I tomb  28–29

Temple of the Plumed Serpent  10–11
temples  4, 6, 10, 11, 14, 18, 29
Teotihuacan  10, 11
Thirty Years' War  24

Valley of the Kings  28
ventilation  6, 20

water  7, 12, 13, 20, 21, 26
wells  7, 12, 13, 20, 24
workshops  4, 12, 13, 22
World War I  25
World War II  12, 23, 24, 25